Johannes Climacus

Or: A Life of Doubt

Johannes Climacus

Or: A Life of Doubt

Søren Kierkegaard

A translation of *De omnibus dubitandum est*
Translated by T.H. Croxhall
Revised and edited by Jane Chamberlain

Library of Congress Catalog Card Number: 00-102183

A catalogue record for this book can be
obtained from the British Library on request

First published in 2001 by
Serpent's Tail,
4 Blackstock Mews,
London N4 2BT

Website: www.serpentstail.com

Set in StoneSerif by Avon Dataset Ltd, Bidford on Avon,
Warwickshire, B50 4JH

Printed in Great Britain by Mackays of Chatham plc

10 9 8 7 6 5 4 3 2 1

Contents

Editor's introduction

Søren Kierkegaard, an indefinable Danish writer who lived and worked in nineteenth-century Copenhagen, put his talents to entertaining use by turning them on his contemporaries who had, he believed, become addicted to an ideal of objective knowledge and the exercise of rationality which smothered all sense of the contingency, uncertainty, and ultimate mystery of human existence. Life had become undemanding – the population complacent, self-satisfied, and anaesthetized by comfort. The people of his time, Kierkegaard wrote, had 'forgotten what it means to *exist.*'

And in this his society reflected the fashionable philosophy of the age – the work of Hegel and his followers, who exalted reason above all else and sought to encompass the whole of history and the cosmos within one great logical system. Kierkegaard ridiculed such conceited philosophers with their delusions of intellectual grandeur, taking delight in puncturing the pretensions of these grand theorists of everything. No human life – not even a philosopher's life – could ever fit into the orderly paragraphs and chapters of systematic philosophy and Hegel was, therefore, 'like a man who builds an enormous castle but lives in a shack nearby.'

Logic and reason have little bearing on the fundamental problems of existence such as those of ethics or religion, and the ideal of objective truth is a chimera peddled by the 'salesmen' of objective thought, who 'translate everything into results' and 'help all mankind to cheat by copying these off and reciting them by rote.' The apparent security of objective knowledge must be relinquished in favour of an authentic acknowledgement that stability is always an illusion – that nothing is ever final because human existence is in constant flux. 'A system of existence cannot be given,' because it is neither an objective fact nor a static state but a *process*, and hence in the realm of subjectivity 'results are only rubbish with which we should not trouble each other,' for 'the truth consists of nothing else than the self-activity of personal appropriation.'

Kierkegaard set out to become, therefore, the most unconventional of philosophical authors. No careful definitions, systematic arguments, or reassuring conclusions will be found in his work but rather a bewildering mosaic of literary genres and forms ranging from essays on Mozart to enigmatic novellas. 'Wherever the subjective is of importance in knowledge, and where appropriation thus constitutes the crux of the matter,' he wrote in his journal, 'the process of communication must be a work of art.' Indeed, much of his work is not published under his own name at all, for he posed (and opposed) a multitude of contrasting and often contradictory ideas through the mouths of pseudonymous or imaginary authors, who are themselves very often little more than mouthpieces for a mad variety of fictional characters speaking with their own voices from his books. By juxtaposing standpoints and ideas in this way, interweaving lifestyles and points of view, Kierkegaard avoids taking an authoritative stand and aims to provoke perplexity in his readers, force them to engage with the problems and difficulties of philosophy and recognize that these are, in fact, their own.

Kierkegaard's novella, *De omnibus dubitandum est* – probably written in the winter of 1842–43, but never completed – tells the story of Johannes Climacus, a dreamy and unassuming young man who lived in a world of his own. Johannes had no interest in girls or in the usual pastimes of youth, for 'thinking is his passion' – he was in love with 'the up-and-down and down-and-up of thought'. Enrolled at university, he listened quietly to the philosophical conversations of others, and in time became attracted to the idea of becoming a philosopher himself. But he was in awe of the subject and remained silent, 'for fear that thinkers of distinction might smile at him if they heard that he too wanted to think.' Yet he listened all the more attentively, and while listening heard again and again the statement that became a 'task for his thinking': *De omnibus dubitandum est* – Everything must be doubted.

Johannes notes that this statement is related to philosophy in some way, and decides to set out on the path to becoming a philosopher by clarifying the connection between philosophy and doubt. He therefore reflects on the three principal theses he has heard concerning the relation between this statement and philosophy:

1. Philosophy begins with doubt.
2. In order to philosophize one must have doubted.
3. Modern philosophy begins with doubt.

He tackled his task energetically, and was often captivated by what he heard from the philosophical company he kept – once becoming so excited by an idea that he 'hastened home happier than Robinson Crusoe when he had found Friday.' But the more he explored these theses, the more discouraged he became, for no matter how far he advanced 'he always arrived at the same point.' He gained nothing from listening to others, except the dawning awareness that attending to their conversation hindered rather than helped his progress, for although they loudly declared that everything must be doubted they clearly had not done so themselves. Eventually, therefore, he resolved to pay them no more attention, since he had had 'so many sad experiences of how deceitful their words were.' He 'said goodbye to these philosophers forever' and decided to go it alone.

Johannes came to doubt the wisdom of these philosophers, then; to suspect that they were only superficially concerned with their subject. And they solemnly declared that everything must be doubted without ever doubting that statement – whereas the declaration that everything must be doubted surely means we must also doubt that everything must be doubted. Earnest young Johannes, by contrast – so engaged with the problem that at one point he faints – not only came to doubt their sincerity, but also to doubt that everything must be doubted: he suspected that 'it was an impossibility', although 'he did not have the courage to believe this'. He doubts *himself*, something else the chattering philosophers never do. The mature Johannes Climacus, though – pseudonymous author of Kierkegaard's *Concluding Unscientific Postscript* – is more assertive:

> If speculative thought, instead of didactically discoursing on *de omnibus dubitandum* and acquiring a chorus of philosophers who swear to swear by *de omnibus dubitandum*, had instead made an attempt to have such a doubter come into existence . . . so that one could see down to the slightest detail how he goes about doing it – well, if it had done this, that is, if it had started to do this, then in turn it would have abandoned it and understood with shame that the grand slogan every parroter swears he has carried out is not only an infinitely difficult task but an impossibility for an existing person.

The obvious response is of course that 'Descartes did it', as another Johannes – this time Johannes *de silentio*, pseudonymous author of Kierkegaard's *Fear and Trembling* – observes. Doubt as a philosophical method, and modern philosophy as such, is said to have begun with Descartes resolving to question all his previous opinions in order to find firm foundations for knowledge, and the 'parrots' young Johannes encountered are the Danish Hegelians of Kierkegaard's time who claimed to have begun by doubting everything and then progressed to the certainties of Hegel's System. But Johannes *de silentio* points out that Descartes was 'a venerable, humble, honest thinker', unlike these pretentious Hegelians with their empty words. Moreover, Descartes took on his task alone – he 'did not shout "Fire! Fire!" and make it obligatory for everyone to doubt'. Most importantly, he did not in fact doubt everything, for 'he did not doubt with respect to faith'.

This was a subject close to Kierkegaard's heart, for nowhere was the superficiality of his society more evident, in his view, than in its attitude towards religious matters. Passionately committed to the Christian faith, yet equally passionate in his hostility to organized Christianity, he poured scorn on the hypocritical or self-deluding tendency of his contemporaries to assume that reciting the right words and attending Church regularly entitled them to call themselves Christian. For him, faith was a wholehearted existential commitment or it was nothing. And the parallel drawn between doubt and faith in the Preface to *Fear and Trembling* is illuminating. The pronouncements of the philosophers Johannes meets were as empty as those of the pseudo-Christians Kierkegaard despised, for philosophy – like faith – is not a set of ideas and doctrines to be memorized and recited by rote but a constant and solitary engagement with the mystery of existence; an intensely personal matter involving the inwardness of the individual alone. Kierkegaard often refers to Hegel's System as an 'omnibus' – literally, a 'vehicle for all'. If *de omnibus dubitandum est*, therefore, what must perhaps be doubted above all is any doctrinal *omnibus* 'that permits everyone to ride along'.

Hence the form of Kierkegaard's text – a narrative of systematic doubt which is anything but systematic, has little narrative progression, and no end. By framing his point obliquely, in a story, he avoids the dangers of direct communication 'which instead of making the reader take an active part makes him hear it like a parrot.' And the indirectness also embodies Kierkegaard's understanding of philosophy as such. Johannes came to understand that doubting everything is not something one person can advise another to do, since the receiver of such advice would have to doubt it: 'When one person said it to another, it became in the latter's hand a sword which must murder the first.' But this holds, too, for the suggestion that the philosophical mysteries of existence must engage each individual alone. In a sense, philosophy is always just beginning, and a truly philosophical life is not a matter of being a philosopher but of trying to become one.

Johannes Climacus

Or: A Life of Doubt

A narrative

'I speak of real doubt existing in the mind, not of such doubt as we see exemplified when a man says that he doubts, though his mind does not really hesitate. The cure of the latter does not fall within the province of method, it belongs rather to inquiries concerning obstinacy and its cure.'

(Spinoza, *On the Improvement of Human Understanding*)

'Let no man despise thy youth.'

I Timothy 4: 12

A satisfaction to note

Someone who supposes that philosophy has never in the world been so near to solving its problems (to explaining all secrets) as now, may well feel it odd, affected, even offensive that I choose the narrative form and do not, in my humble way, lend a hand with putting the coping stone on the System. On the other hand, someone who has convinced himself that philosophy has never been so eccentric as now, so confused, in spite of all its definitions, so very like the weather last winter when all at the same time we heard what had never before been heard, shouts of mussels and prawns and watercress in such a way that someone who attended to a particular shout might at one time think it was winter, at another time spring, at another time midsummer, while someone who paid attention to all these shouts at once might think that nature had become confused and the world could not last till Easter – they will certainly think it right that I should also, by means of the form, try to counteract the detestable falsity which is the mark of modern philosophy; a philosophy which is distinguished from older philosophy by its discovery of the ridiculousness of doing what one said one did or had done – they will find it appropriate and will only be sorry, as I am, that the person who begins this task has not greater authority than I have.

Introduction

In the city of H. . . . . there lived some years ago a young
student by the name of Johannes Climacus, whose desire
was by no means to become prominent in the world, for
on the contrary it was his joy to live apart, concealed, and
in quietness. Those who knew him at all closely tried to
explain his enclosed nature (which shunned close contact
with people) by assuming that he was either melancholy or
in love. Those who thought the latter were in a sense not
wrong; though they were indeed mistaken if they supposed
that the object of his dreams was a girl. Such feelings were
totally alien to his heart, and just as his external
appearance was refined and ethereal, almost transparent,
so his soul was correspondingly far too intellectual and
spiritual to be captivated by a woman's beauty. In love he
was, ardently in love – but with thought or, more
accurately, with thinking. No young lover, stirred by that
incomprehensible transition whereby love wakens in his
breast, by the lightning flash with which reciprocal love
bursts forth in the beloved, could be more deeply moved
than he was by that comprehensible transition whereby
one thought fits with another. Such a transition was for
him the happy moment in which there was brought to pass
what he had suspected and hoped for in the silence of his

soul. When, therefore, his head was bowed like a ripe ear of corn, it was not because he heard the voice of his beloved, but because he was listening to the secret whispering of his thoughts; when his glance was dreamy, this was not because he was thinking of her image but because the movement of thought was becoming visible to him. It was his delight to begin with a single thought, and from that to climb up step by step to a higher one along the path of logical inference; for logical inference formed his *Scala Paradisi*, and his bliss was to him more glorious than that of the angels. When he had reached a higher thought it was an indescribable joy, a passionate delight for him to plunge headlong down the same inferences till he reached the point from which he had started. Things did not, however, always go as he wished. If in his descent he did not receive precisely the same number of bumps as there were links in the inferences, he became despondent, for then the movements must have been imperfect. He would therefore start all over again. If he succeeded, his soul would thrill with delight, he could not sleep at night and would continue for hours on end making the same movements, for this up-and-down and down-and-up of thought was an unparalleled joy. In those successful times his going was easy, almost floating; at other times it was troubled and unsteady. When climbing up was a labour to him, it meant that logical inference had as yet not been able to make progress, and this would depress him. For he feared to lose all the conclusions he had arrived at, even if they had not as yet become fully perspicuous to him and inevitable. When we see someone carrying a load of breakable things stacked one upon the other, we are not surprised that he walks unsteadily and is constantly trying to keep his balance. But if we do not see the pile, we smile. Thus many people smiled at Johannes, not suspecting that his soul was carrying a far higher pile than would normally cause surprise, and that he was anxious lest a single one of the logical inferences should tumble and the whole pile fall to pieces. He did not notice that people smiled at him, no more than at other times he noticed some cheerful soul turn round and look at him when he hastened through the streets lightly as in a dance. He paid no heed to other people, and never imagined they might pay heed to him. He was and remained a stranger in the world.

But if Climacus's character must have seemed odd to anybody not knowing him well, it was by no means inexplicable to someone with a little knowledge of his earlier life, for he was to a large extent still the same now, in his twenty-first year, as he had always been. His natural disposition had not been disturbed in his childhood, but had developed in favourable circumstances. His home did not offer many diversions, and since he very rarely went out he became from his early years accustomed to being occupied with himself and his own thoughts. His father was a very stern man, to all appearances dry and prosaic, but under his 'rustic cloak' manner he concealed an ardent imagination which not even his great age could blunt. When on occasion Johannes asked permission to go out, as often as not he was refused; though once in a while his father would suggest by way of compensation that his son should take his hand and go for a walk up and down the

room. At first blush this seemed a poor substitute; and yet,
just as with that 'rustic cloak' manner, there was more
behind it than appeared. The offer was accepted, and
Johannes was given completely free choice as to where they
should go. They walked out of the city gate to a nearby
country castle, or away to the beach, or about the streets,
or wherever Johannes wished, for the father was equal to
anything. While they walked up and down the room the
father would describe everything they saw. They greeted
the passers-by; the carriages rattled by them and drowned
the father's voice; the cake-woman's wares were more
inviting than ever. The father would describe so accurately,
so vividly, so faithfully – even down to the most
insignificant detail – what was already known to Johannes,
and so forthrightly and graphically what was unknown to
him, that after half an hour's walking with his father he
was as overcome and weary as if he had been out for a
whole day. Johannes soon learned his father's magic power.
Then what had been an epic became a drama, and
dialogues were held on the journey. If they walked along
familiar ways, they each kept a sharp watch over the other
to see that nothing was overlooked. If the way was
unfamiliar to Johannes, he would make associations, while
his father's almighty imagination was able to construct
anything, using every childish fancy as an ingredient in
the drama taking place. For Johannes it was as if the world
came into existence as they conversed, as if his father was
God and he himself God's favoured one who was permitted
to interpose his poor conceits as merrily as he liked. For he
was never rebutted and his father was never nonplussed –

everything was included, and always to Johannes's satisfaction.

While the life in his paternal home thus contributed to the development of his imagination – teaching him to enjoy the taste of ambrosia – the education he received in school was in harmony with this. The high authority of Latin grammar and the divine status of rules encouraged a new infatuation. But it was Greek grammar that specially attracted him – so much so that he forgot to read Homer aloud to himself as he had been wont to do in order to enjoy the rhythms of the poem. His Greek teacher taught grammar in a somewhat philosophical way. When it was explained to Johannes that the accusative case, for example, implies extension in time and space, or that it is not the preposition but the relationship that governs the case, then new vistas opened out to his mind. The preposition disappeared, and extension in time and space became like a huge empty picture for his intuition. His imagination was once again set in motion, but in a different way than before. What had entertained him on his walks was the filled space which he could not get around himself tightly enough. His imagination was so productive that it could make do with very little. Outside the only window in the living room there grew about ten blades of grass, where he would sometimes discover a little creature running between the stems. These blades became a huge forest, which had all the denseness and darkness that this grass had. But instead of that filled space he now had the empty space; he gazed again, but saw nothing except the enormous expanse.

Søren Kierkegaard

While thus there was being developed in him an almost
vegetative tendency to drowse in imagination – partly
aesthetic, partly intellectual – another side of his soul was
being strongly formed, namely his sense for the sudden,
the surprising. This did not come about through those
magic means which usually serve to rivet children's
attention, but through something far higher. With his
almighty imagination the father combined an irresistible
dialectic. When on any occasion his father engaged in an
argument with somebody, Johannes was all ears; the more
so because everything was conducted with an almost
festive decorum. His father always allowed his opponent to
state his whole case, and then would ask him very carefully
whether he had anything more to say before he began his
reply. Johannes, having followed the opponent's speech
with keen attention, shared in his measure an interest in
the outcome. Then came the pause, the father's rejoinder
would follow, and look! – in a twinkling everything was
changed. How this happened remained a riddle to
Johannes, but his soul delighted in this drama. The
opponent would speak again, and Johannes would be still
more attentive so that he should miss nothing. His father
would then perorate, and Johannes could almost hear his
heart beat, so impatiently did he await what should
happen. It did happen! In an instant everything would be
inverted; what was clear became obscure, what was certain
doubtful, the opposite became self-evident. When a shark
wants to seize its prey, it must turn over on its back, for its
mouth is on its belly side; its back is dark, its belly silvery
white. What a glorious sight it must be to see this

20

alternation in colour; it must sometimes twinkle so much as almost to hurt the eye, and yet be a delight to look upon. Such was the kind of alternation Johannes witnessed when he heard his father in debate. He soon forgot what was said, both by his father and the opponent, but this thrill in his soul he never forgot. Analogous experiences in his school-life were not lacking. He saw how a word could alter a whole sentence, how a subjunctive in the midst of an indicative sentence could throw new light on the whole. The older he grew, and the more intimate his father became with him, the more conscious he became of that inexplicable quality. It was as if his father had a secret understanding of what Johannes wanted to say, and therefore could confuse everything for him by a single word. When his father was not simply opposing him, but putting forward some thesis of his own, Johannes observed how he proceeded; how he made his point in successive stages. This taught him to suspect that the reason his father could turn everything upside down with a word must be that he, Johannes, had forgotten something in the sequence of thought.

What other children obtain through the magic of poetry and the surprise of fairy tales, Johannes obtained through quiet intuition and the ramifications of dialectic. Herein was the child's delight, became the boy's play, the youth's desire. Hence his life was characterized by an unusual continuity; it knew nothing of the various transitions which usually indicate different stages of growth. When Johannes grew older he had no toys to lay aside, for he had learnt to play with that which was to be the serious business of his life.

And yet this never lost its attraction. A little girl plays for so long with her doll that at last it is transformed into her beloved, for woman's whole life is love. His life had a similar continuity, for his whole life was thinking.

Johannes became a university student, passed his second examination, reached the age of twenty, and still there was no change in him – he was and remained a stranger in the world. Nevertheless he did not shun people; on the contrary he tried to meet people of like mind to himself. But he did not speak his mind freely, or allow people to know what went on inside him – his love was too deep for that. It was as if he must blush if he talked about it, and he was afraid to know too much or too little. On the other hand, he always took notice of what others said. Just as a young girl deeply in love does not readily talk about her love, but with an almost painful tension listens hard when other girls talk about theirs (for she wants to test in silence whether she is as happy, or even happier than they, and will snatch at any little hint that will guide her), so Johannes took notice of everything. And when he got home he reflected on what the philosophizers had said, for of course it was their company he had sought.

But it never occurred to him to want to be a philosopher, or dedicate himself to Speculation; he was still too fickle for that. True, he was not drawn now to one thing and now to another – thinking was and remained his passion – but he still lacked the self-discipline required for acquiring a deeper coherence. Both the significant and the insignificant attracted him equally as points of departure

for his pursuits; the result was not of great consequence –
only the movements of thought as such interested him.
Sometimes he noticed that he reached one and the same
conclusion from quite different starting points, but this
did not in any deeper sense engage his attention. His
delight was always just to be pressing on; wherever he
suspected a labyrinth, he had to find the way. Once he had
started, nothing could bring him to a halt. If he found the
going difficult and became tired of it before he ought, he
would adopt a very simple remedy – he would shut himself
up in his room, make everything as festive as possible, and
then say loudly and clearly: I *will* do it. He had learned
from his father that one can do what one wills, and his
father's life had not discredited this theory. Experiencing
this had given Johannes indescribable pride; that there
could be something one could not do when one willed it
was unbearable to him. But his pride did not in the least
indicate weakness of will, for when he had uttered these
energetic words he was ready for anything; he then had a
still higher goal – to penetrate the intricacies of the
problem by force of will. This again was an adventure that
inspired him. Indeed his life was in this way always
adventurous. He needed no woods and wanderings for his
adventures, but only what he possessed – a little room with
one window.

Although his soul was therefore from his early years led out
towards ideality, this in no way weakened his faith and
confidence in actuality. The ideality upon which he had
been nourished was so close to him, and everything went so
naturally, that this ideality became his actuality, and in

turn he expected to find ideality in the actuality outside
himself. His father's melancholy contributed to this. That
the father was an extraordinary man was a thing that
Johannes at last came to realize. That the father astonished
him as no other person did to the same degree, the son
knew. But he knew so few people that he had no yardstick
by which to measure. That his father, humanly speaking,
was extraordinary, he did not learn in the paternal house.
Once in a while when an old and trusted friend visited the
family, and engaged in a more confidential conversation
with the father, Johannes often heard him say, 'I am good
for nothing. I can do nothing. My only wish is to find a
place in some charitable institution.' He was not joking.
There were no traces of irony in his father's words. On the
contrary there was a dark seriousness about them which
made Johannes anxious. Neither was this a casual remark,
for the father was capable of proving that the most
insignificant person in the world was a genius compared
with himself. No counter-proof was of any avail, for his
irresistible dialectic could make one forget what was most
obvious and compel one to be transfixed by the view he had
put forward as though there were no other in the world.
Johannes, whose whole outlook on life was, so to speak,
bound up in his father (for he saw so little else) became
caught in a contradiction, because it escaped him for a long
time that his father contradicted himself – not least through
the virtuosity with which he could crush every opponent
and reduce them to silence. Johannes's confidence in
actuality then was not weakened; he had not imbibed
ideality from books which teach those they nurture that the

glory they describe is not to be found in this world. He was not educated by a man who knew how to make his knowledge seem precious, but rather by one who knew how to make it seem as insignificant and worthless as possible.

Part one

Johannes Climacus begins to philosophize with the help of traditional conceptions

Introduction

Although he had been at the University for some years, Johannes had read relatively little, especially for a student. He had a very good acquaintance with the ancient and classical writers whom he had read at his grammar school, and it was a joy to him to go through them again from time to time, though their contents did not touch the deep stirrings of his own heart. Occasionally modern books of this or that sort would come into his hands, but he had no clear idea about what significance the reading of them should have for him. Historical works did not interest him greatly, because the prevailing trend of his mind had divested him of any feeling for empirical actuality, and just as he was usually indifferent to what other people said or did if it had no relation to thinking, so he was indifferent to information about what people who had lived earlier had said or done. If he came across a book of modern philosophy he did not of course put it aside before he had read it, but when he had read it he was often dissatisfied and dejected. His whole trend of mind made him uncomfortable about reading. Sometimes the title tempted him; then he would go to the volume happy and full of expectations. But look! It would deal with many irrelevant things and say very little about what one would have expected. If, after some struggle, he eventually got through to what the title had justified him in looking for, then often the reasoning was interrupted and the matter left in the air. What often struck him was the way that so much attention was given to things that seemed to him quite incidental. The investigation would be interrupted in order to correct some abstruse opinion or other, held by some author quite unknown to him. Rightly to understand such a digression really required that he should have read the other person's works. Perhaps this in turn presupposed others, and so on. He thought he detected too that the reason a certain author's opinion was attended to was very peculiar; for example, that he lived in the same town as the writer, or wrote in the same journal, or other things of that sort. He did not always find strict dialectical movement; he sadly missed the wondrous delights of dialectic and its mysterious surprises. After several attempts, he would give up reading and deliver himself over once more to his own thoughts, even though they led to nothing. Meantime he had refrained from any over-hasty judgements about these particular books, or about books in general. He heard others make quite different assessments of them, and concluded that the fault lay in him, that his upbringing had been imperfect, and that if it had taught him nothing else, it had at least taught him to draw this conclusion.

By paying heed to the conversation of others, he realized that he had not come across the writings of the great thinkers among recent philosophers. Again and again he heard their names mentioned with enthusiasm, almost with reverence. This gave him indescribable joy, even though he did not venture to read them because he had heard that they were so difficult that the study of them took ages. It was not cowardice or indolence that stopped him, but a painful feeling which had pursued him from his early childhood that he was not like other people. He was far from feeling happy about this difference; on the contrary he felt it as a load under which he would have to suffer all his life. He felt like a child who was born into the world with much pain, and who could not forget this pain, though the mother had forgotten it for joy at his birth.

As regards his reading, Johannes found himself in a curious dilemma. The books he knew did not satisfy him, but he did not dare blame this on the writings themselves; outstanding works he did not venture to read. So he read less and less, followed his inclination to muse in silence, became more and more retiring for fear that thinkers of distinction might smile at him when they heard that he too wanted to think, just as distinguished ladies smile at a poor girl when she too presumes to want the experience of love's bliss. He was silent, but listened all the more attentively.

When he heard others talking, he noticed that one particular thought would crop up again and again. He seized upon this and made it the object of his thinking. Thus Fate came to his aid by procuring material for him in precisely the way he needed. The purer and so-to-say more virgin-like his problem was, the more he loved it; the less others had helped him forward with his thoughts, the happier he was, and the better everything went for him. He seemed to consider it an imperfection that he could best think a thought when it came to him like newly fallen snow, without having gone through the hands of others. He regarded it as a great thing to be able, as were the others, to romp about among the manifold thoughts of manifold thinkers, but he soon forgot this pain in the joy of thinking.

By listening to others talking, he became particularly aware of one statement which came up again and again, was passed from mouth to mouth and was always eulogized, always revered. Many times he heard it repeated, *De omnibus dubitandum est*: 'Everything must be doubted.' He clung to this statement and it came to play a decisive role in his life. It became for his life what a name often is in the story of any person's life – by mentioning this name you sum up everything.

This statement became a task for his thinking. Whether it would take a long or a short time to think it through he did not know, but one thing he knew – that he would not give up before that moment, even if it should cost him his life.

What excited him even more was the relationship usually assumed between this statement and becoming a philosopher. Whether he would ever be able to become a philosopher he did not know, but he would try his best. With quiet solemnity it was decreed that he should begin. He edified himself by recalling the enthusiasm of Dion who said, when he embarked with but a few men to begin the war with Dionysius: 'It is enough for me that I have taken part. If I should die the moment I set foot on land, without having achieved anything, I will still regard this death as fortunate and glorious.'

Johannes now set to work to get clear in his mind the relation between this statement and philosophy. To occupy himself thus would be an encouraging prelude to philosophy proper; the clearer he became about this, the more enthusiastically would he proceed to the main concern. So he closed himself up in himself with this philosophical statement, paying careful attention meanwhile to every clue he could glean. If he noticed that his own process of thought was different from that of others, he stamped theirs on his memory, went home and began again. That their thought process was generally very short did, of course, strike him, but he saw that only as a new point to their advantage.

So he began his operations, and immediately juxtaposed the three main theses he had heard concerning the relationship of this statement to philosophy. These three theses were as follows: (1) Philosophy begins with doubt. (2) In order to philosophize one must have doubted. (3) Modern philosophy begins with doubt.

Chapter one

Modern philosophy begins with doubt

What immediately struck him about these three theses was that they seemed by no means homogeneous. While the first two must in the strict sense, because of their universality, be regarded as philosophical – for they stated something universal about the philosophy of all times and all places, or about the philosophizer of all times and places – the third seemed to be a historical report that must first undergo a transformation before it could claim in a strict sense to be of a philosophical nature. Historically, of course, it could be interesting to know that modern philosophy begins with doubt, in the same way as it could be interesting to know whether it begins in Germany or in France, and with whom. If on the other hand a transformation did take place, then it probably could be subsumed under one of the foregoing theses.

In order to check whether this might be possible, he decided to explore the thesis in more detail.

1. How must the thesis be understood literally?

Here he strove to assess what significance there might be in adding to 'philosophy' the adjective 'modern' – which, of course, is a historical predicate. The thesis was, therefore, merely asserting something about a particular historical philosophy. He accepted the thesis as true, for he had neither reading nor maturity enough to investigate this for himself. It followed from the thesis that there had been an older philosophy which had not begun in the same way; for were this not so the thesis would be very imperfectly expressed. He then asked whether he would be justified in concluding that a later philosophy could begin in yet another way, thus implying that philosophy could begin in various ways and yet continue to be philosophy. In order to be as brief as possible, he asked whether a later philosophy could in turn begin in the same way as that older philosophy and yet be philosophy; or whether, after modern philosophy had begun with doubt, this would have a decisive influence on the whole future. If this were so, would it also have retroactive power, so that the extent to which that older philosophy could be called philosophy would become doubtful, despite the fact that it began with something else? In other words, if modern philosophy, because of its beginning, has excluded for all future time the possibility of another beginning, this suggests that this beginning is more than a historical beginning, is an essential beginning. In that case, modern philosophy is essential philosophy, and to call that older version philosophy is only an accommodation – if the words are understood in this way, then the thesis has undergone a transformation by which it becomes identical with the first thesis, that philosophy begins with doubt.

Whether this was the position of philosophy itself, he did not know. He sought in vain for some illuminative clue in the conversation of others. If this was the position, then it seemed odd to him that people expressed themselves so imprecisely, that they confused historical and eternal categories in such a way that when they seemed to say something historical they said something eternal. Why not confine oneself to the first thesis, that philosophy begins with doubt? For then nothing is doubtful, then everything that does not begin with doubt, whatever it may be, is not philosophy. True enough, this would have the strange result that this eternal beginning began in time, in such a way that there had been times in which it had not begun, whereas he imagined that the eternal beginning existed at all times. If he had understood correctly, it had caused philosophy great difficulty that Christianity said that it had come into the world by a beginning that was simultaneously historical and eternal; it must, then, be risky for philosophy to want to assert the same about itself.

From yet another angle Johannes made the words of the thesis the object of deliberation. The thesis says modern *philosophy* – it does not speak of a particular philosopher who is historically reported to have begun by doubting, it speaks of modern philosophy as a whole. No past tense is used, or even a historical present such as one uses when one says 'Descartes begins with doubt', thereby indicating something past which is present only in the historical narrative. One uses an eternal present, as if modern philosophy is also something more than a particular philosopher. To that extent, the thesis seems to say something more than something merely historical. We must suppose it does this for another reason as well. Modern philosophy must, of course, be assumed to be always in the process of becoming, otherwise there would always be something more modern in relation to which it would be older. Is it not conceivable that modern philosophy, as it extended and grew, became aware of its wrong beginning, which then, regarded as a beginning, would prove to be no beginning at all? By what authority is this beginning declared a beginning for the whole of modern philosophy? This can only be right if the beginning itself is the essential beginning for modern philosophy, but this, historically speaking, can only be decided when all modern philosophy is concluded. If it is to be asserted before that time, then it must be said and understood eternally – in other words, it must be because this beginning is the essential beginning for all philosophy. In that case, the thesis has again undergone a transformation whereby it becomes identical with the first thesis, that philosophy begins with doubt.

Why then did philosophy use two expressions, one of which either says the same as the other and is, in that case, incorrect; or else it says something different and is, if this be assumed, obscure?

Although the ambiguity of the thesis, as he had now come to regard it, might have made him uneasy about proceeding further, nevertheless he decided to examine what the thesis might mean if he assumed for the time being that it was a historical thesis. As such it was, then, different from the first thesis, and his only choice was to suppose either that it was completely superfluous and could only lead to confusion, or that it was a historical thesis somewhat oddly expressed.

2. How did it come about that modern philosophy began with doubt?

Johannes assumed that modern philosophy began with doubt, and now asked how this had come about, whether it was by accident or by necessity, whether this beginning was an accidental one or a necessary one.

(a) *Was it by accident that modern philosophy began with doubt?*

Here Johannes asked whether it was the same kind of accident as that by which purple was discovered – an accident of such a kind that to all eternity it would remain an accident. If the thesis 'Modern philosophy begins with doubt' is like that, then it refers to a historical accident from which no conclusion can be drawn about either past or future philosophy, or about philosophy in general, just as you cannot conclude from what happened to the dog which discovered purple that every dog must discover purple. If the thesis be like that, it contains a piece of merely historical information, but then it contradicts the first thesis, that philosophy begins with doubt, for if these theses are juxtaposed it becomes evident that the essential happened by accident.

Next he asked whether the accident by which modern

philosophy came to begin with doubt was perhaps of such a
kind that it concealed a necessity within itself – a necessity
which in the next moment explained the accident; whether
this accident was like the accident by which Newton
discovered the law of gravitation, for although that was an
accident, yet the law it discovered at once made it clear that
the accident itself was a necessity. If that was so then it
would only appear to be the case – in an imperfect
historical sense – that modern philosophy had by accident
begun with doubt, for in the same moment modern
philosophy would discover the necessity of its beginning in
that way. But modern philosophy, as a historical event,
could not yet have discovered this necessity, because
modern philosophy is not yet concluded. If then this
necessity were to be discovered, it would be in an eternal
sense, because modern philosophy is philosophy in general.
Such a discovery would have to be decisive for the future,
and retrospective towards the past, with regard to the
question of the beginning of philosophy. To that extent, the
thesis would have undergone a transformation whereby it
would become identical with the first thesis.

(b) *Was it by necessity that modern philosophy began with
doubt?*
Johannes now asked about the nature of that which
preceded modern philosophy, that which had made it
necessary for modern philosophy to begin with doubt. Was
this a philosophy or something else? To this question he
answered that according to the statement's own words it
must be a philosophy. What kind of philosophy then must it
have been, to make it necessary for modern philosophy to

begin with doubt? Was that philosophy, which by its
precedence had made it necessary for modern philosophy to
begin with doubt, was that philosophy and modern
philosophy alone philosophy, so that if there had existed
before in the world a philosophy which had begun in some
other way, it must accept that it was not philosophy? And
had that preceding philosophy begun by accident or by
necessity? So as not to be led too far afield, he sought to
account for the following: if modern philosophy by
necessity begins with doubt, then its beginning must be
defined in continuity with an earlier philosophy. If, therefore,
we want to say something historical about what philosophy
begins with, we must presumably mention that with which
the antecedent philosophy began, because the beginning of
modern philosophy would only be a consequence within an
earlier beginning. (This supposition would, of course, have a
disturbing effect on the first thesis, that philosophy begins
with doubt.) At once, however, Johannes perceived the
difficulty here which he would have to deal with later –
namely, that such a consequence would be difficult to think,
because the beginning with which modern philosophy began
was defined as a break. It must then be a unique kind of
consequence – namely, a consequence by which one thing
produces its opposite. This is usually called a leap.

Meantime, however, Johannes clung as best he could to the
thought that it was by a necessary consequence that modern
philosophy began with doubt. He concluded, therefore, that
modern philosophy's beginning must be an essential
beginning for philosophy, since one certainly could not be
justified – except merely historically and accidentally – in

asserting something essential about a process which is not yet concluded. It might, after all, become apparent afterwards that the beginning was not a beginning to anything at all, but a misunderstanding, and therefore least of all a beginning to a philosophy. The beginning philosopher could never be justified in saying: With me begins modern philosophy; nor would the sanction of his successor be adequate either, unless the declaration itself was something essential about all philosophy. If the thesis is to be understood in this way, then once again it is transformed and resembles the first thesis.

3. Foreboding

With all these deliberations, Johannes had not advanced one step. This pained him. He could not make up his mind to assume that the third and first theses were identical, for he had no confidence in such a confusing tautology. Confusing it was, because it encouraged people to think of something as different when it was in fact the same. If the same thing was meant by both propositions, then the tautology was confusing. He could not maintain the difference without making a little change, by which the thesis became a historical insignificance, as though one said 'Descartes began with doubt and many others followed his example'. There can be no objection, philosophically speaking, to such a statement. If it presents difficulties, these must be of a historical kind such as, for example, whether it was really true that they themselves had said that they had done it, and whether they had done what they said they had done.

In vain did Johannes hope that by listening to the conversation of others he would get some elucidation – in vain. They used the first and third sentences as totally identical; sometimes they said the one, sometimes the other, sometimes both at once. Sometimes one person would use the one sentence in the course of conversation, and another person would answer him with the other sentence, and they understood each other and understood that they were saying the same thing. The thesis was not clarified, yet clarity was what Johannes really needed, and his own private thinking had made him more receptive to the guidance of others. Yet clarification was not forthcoming; on the contrary, the thesis was sometimes repeated so quickly by the speakers that he almost became dizzy from the very monotony of it. Then he would always return home troubled, for what others found so easy that they merely had to throw it out casually, he found very difficult to think.

He thought through the thesis again and again, tried to forget what he had thought in order to begin again, but lo and behold, he always arrived at the same point. Yet he could not abandon the thesis; it was as though a mysterious power captivated him, as though something whispered to him: 'There is something hiding behind this misunderstanding.' He now tried to combine what he had separated, when he had thought that the thesis must be either a purely philosophical one or purely historical. He thought – it is indeed a mystery that modern philosophy is at once historical and eternal, and what is more, is aware of this itself. It is a union like the union of the two natures in Christ. With every step that modern philosophy takes, it becomes conscious of its eternal significance, or rather it becomes conscious of this before it takes the step, for it could be thought that the step was such that it never could acquire eternal significance unless the historical advance of philosophy was absolutely identical with the Idea's own movement. But in that case the step forward would not be a historical one. Modern philosophy would not then need to undergo any transformation, any retroactive transfiguration, any purification of forgetfulness, in order to be taken up into the System, but down to the most insignificant detail would slot straight into the System, just as a historical personage who was so poetic that his every word, his every gesture was pure poetry, would not need to undergo any transformation in order to go on to the stage but could go straight there from the street just as he is, and without the slightest embarrassment.

It still was not clear to Johannes, however, how he was to think such a combination. His anguished soul full of unrest and foreboding, he suspected that this must be something extraordinary, that to be a philosopher nowadays must be something indescribably difficult. If modern philosophy was like this, it must be the same for the individual philosopher. The individual philosopher *must become conscious of himself; and in this consciousness of himself also become conscious of his significance as a factor (moment) in modern philosophy; then modern philosophy must in turn become conscious of itself as a factor in a preceding philosophy; which in turn must become conscious of itself as a factor in the historical unfolding of the eternal philosophy*. The consciousness of the philosopher must, therefore, encompass the most dizzying contrasts – on the one hand his own personality, his little contribution, and on the other hand the philosophy of the whole world as the unfolding of the eternal philosophy.

It was a long time before Johannes could think this tremendous thought correctly and definitely. Just as a man rolling a heavy load up a mountain is often overcome so that his foot slips and his load rolls down, so it went with him. At last he was sure of himself and could make the movement with ease. He then decided to let the thought work with all its weight, for he made a distinction between the difficulty of thinking and the weight of the thought. As a historical thought, he could think it with ease. He had gathered new strength, felt vigorous; he put himself well under the idea and look – it overwhelmed him and *he fainted*. When he came to he scarcely dared turn his attention to that thought. It occurred to him that it could drive someone mad, at least someone who was no stronger in nerves than he. How much greater then was his' admiration of those who were able to think such things as easily as if it were all child's play!

He became discouraged. But even as he was lapsing into discouragement, he felt caught again, almost against his will, by that immense thought. He was too troubled to actually think properly, but it occurred to him that this thought, which seemed so extremely positive, was really a scepticism, since the individual's knowledge was only ever a knowledge of himself merely as a factor and of his significance as a factor. Assuming this was actually possible, something he could not rightly grasp, then it was not clear to him how a factor could become conscious of itself merely as a factor, for this consciousness was an impossibility without a consciousness that was more than a consciousness of itself as a factor, because otherwise my consciousness must reside in another – this knowledge would then become entirely relative and would by no means be an absolute knowledge. But how is it possible that every single factor can become conscious of its eternal validity as a factor in the whole? The individual would have to be omniscient to see this, and the world be finished.

That the single individual could become conscious of the eternal, he could perhaps grasp, and an earlier philosophy had presumably thought so too – if there had been such a thing. But to become conscious of the eternal in the whole panorama of concrete history, and measuring too not only by the past, this he believed was reserved for the deity. Nor could he grasp at what point in time a person became so transfigured that he could, although present to himself, become past to himself. He believed that this must be reserved for eternity, and that eternity is only present in time in an abstract sense.

Insofar as there had been an earlier philosophy, then, any individual philosopher would presumably have also made use of his precursors, would have seen that he could appropriate this, correct that, and so on, but it probably would not occur to him to want to see the eternal necessity by which one philosopher emerged from another and he himself from his predecessors in an eternal continuity. Even though one might succeed in perceiving such an inner necessity by considering the past (please note that the more distant the past, the greater the possibility of deception), with regard to the present this seemed to him an impossibility. The present was not given leave to become a present out of zeal that it should (the sooner the better) become a past, for in this way it would become neither. This he saw clearly by considering personal life. When one looks back over one's life it may, especially the earlier part of it, appear to be permeated by necessity. On the other hand, if someone on beginning a particular phase of his life first wants to become conscious of this in its eternal validity as a factor in his life, then he will certainly prevent it from acquiring significance, for he will annul it before it has been by wanting that which is a present to manifest itself in the same instant as a past.

It was, it seemed to him, always a precarious thing to undertake to prophesy. And yet, just as one can assume a necessity in the past, one can equally well imagine it being assumed in the future. What philosophy tries to do, however, is something far more difficult, namely to permeate everything with the thought of eternity and necessity, and to do this in the present moment, which is to murder the present with the thought of eternity and yet preserve its life fresh. It wants to see what is happening as that which has happened and yet at the same time as that which is happening, it wants to know the future as a present and yet at the same time as a future.

So far had Johannes come through reflecting on that thesis. It had not happened as quickly as it is here related. It had cost him time and diligence, but he was poorly rewarded for his trouble, for if he were to have an opinion about the thesis under discussion it was this – that it was an impossibility. Yet he had not the courage to believe this.

Chapter two

Philosophy begins with doubt

Johannes first juxtaposed this thesis with thesis number two, that in order to philosophize one must have doubted. He easily saw that they did not say the same thing, for while the first defined doubt as the beginning of philosophy, the second defined doubt as something which preceded the beginning. He had fixed his attention on these three theses because, among other things, they might shed light on the connection between the statement *de omnibus dubitandum est* and philosophy, and thereby make his prospects of being brought to philosophize more or less brighter. Naturally therefore thesis number one pleased him, for it seemed to be the quickest way. It did not speak of doubt as something preceding philosophy; it taught that in doubt one was at the beginning of philosophy.

1. Is the thesis identical with thesis number three?

Johannes found it a curious idea that doubt should be an integral part of philosophy. It seemed to him that what happened with thesis number one was the opposite of what happened with thesis number three. This seemed to be a

historical sentence, but it turned out on closer inspection
that it must be a philosophical one, even though he could
not understand it as such. Thesis number one appeared at
first sight to be a philosophical sentence, since it speaks of
philosophy in general, but on closer examination it seemed
historical. It states that philosophy begins with a negative
principle, and this principle contains a polemic against not
merely this or that which is outside philosophy, but against
a principle within philosophy itself. Since it would of course
be absurd to polemicize against nothing, this presupposes
an antecedent. If this antecedent is not a principle, then the
polemic is unworthy of philosophy – indeed the thesis
would not then be negative but positive, for if in my
polemic I merely exclude the heterogeneous, then my thesis
is not really a polemic one but a statement of something
higher that I have. But the thesis cannot be unaware of this
polemic against something homogenous, for while a
positive principle, as immediate, can be unaware of what it
excludes, a negative principle never could be. The thesis
itself, therefore, concedes an antecedent philosophical
principle.

Had it been a positive principle with which philosophy
began, one could certainly not deduce from this any
historical consequences. As far as Johannes knew, the Greeks
taught that philosophy begins with wonder. Such a principle
cannot give rise to any historical consequences at all. If a
later thinker made the same assumption, one could not
justifiably conclude from this that he thought one should
begin with wonder at the fact that Plato and Aristotle had
wondered. Wonder is clearly an immediate category, and

involves no reflection upon itself. Doubt, on the other hand, is a reflection-category. If a later philosopher said 'Philosophy begins with wonder', he was straightaway in continuity with the Greeks. They had wondered, he wonders also; they had perhaps wondered at one thing, he at another. But whenever a later philosopher repeats or utters the words 'Philosophy begins with doubt', the continuity is broken, for doubt is precisely a polemic against what has gone before. The more important the person who repeats the thesis, the more gaping is the break; while in the other case the more important the person repeating the thesis, the more it is confirmed and strengthened. It is true that in the first case the thesis is also strengthened by repetition, but it is strengthened specifically in order to separate.

The more he thought the thesis through, the more it showed itself to be a historical thesis and identical with thesis number three, so that once again, though by a reverse process, he reached just the same position as before. Yet this was not all; he discovered a new difficulty too. That an individual could take it into his head to doubt, Johannes could well conceive. But he could not understand how it could occur to anyone to say this to another person, least of all as advice (it would be a different matter if he were trying to put him off), for unless the other person were exceedingly slow, he might very well answer, 'Thank you very much, but you must forgive me if I now also doubt the correctness of that statement.' Now if the first speaker, out of joy at the other's gratitude, were to tell a third person that he and the other were in agreement about doubting everything, then he would really be making a fool of the third person, since their agreement was only a completely abstract expression for their disagreement – unless they were so impolite as to regard each other as nothing, which would be a new contradiction, since the person who first advanced the thesis must certainly have regarded himself as something, and must have regarded the second person as something too, since he wanted to initiate him into it. Nor could the first person be angry over the conduct of the second, for he could hardly want him to be a more imperfect character than himself and, above all, he could not want the second to be inconsistent, any more than in antiquity Anaxarchus, who had fallen into a deep ditch, could become angry with Pyrrho for passing him by without helping him out, but on the contrary praised him for doing as he did, since it proved that they were truly agreed that a philosopher ought to be indifferent and unsympathetic.

Although Johannes could certainly grasp all this, yet his mentality was such that he had not the courage to be consistent like this with regard to truths which others applauded. Even if it would be inconsistent of a genius to want to demand this of someone, it was nevertheless consistent of a poor student to do so. Of course he realized the imperfection in his way of appropriating truth, but he would not on that account let go of the thesis. So he tried to think it over again in order to see how he could enter into relation with it. It was not as yet the thesis itself he wanted to think through, for first he must know whether he could successfully enter into a relation with it. Hence he did not ask such questions as: Is doubt, as the beginning, a part of

philosophy or is it the whole of philosophy? If it is a part,
what then is the other part? Is this certainty? Are these parts
sundered to all eternity? How can we speak of a whole if its
parts are mutually exclusive? What Epicurus had said in his
sophistical way about the fear of death seemed relevant here
– namely, that we ought not to concern ourselves about it,
for when I am, death is not, and when death is, I am not. Is
there anything that might unite the two parts into a whole?
Johannes did not ask such questions as these, but only asked
about the single individual's relation to that thesis.

2. How does the single individual relate to that thesis?

While his soul was pregnantly pondering this question (as
long as he could not ask questions, thought twined itself
alarmingly around him, but as soon as he began to ask
questions he was happy, for then he extricated himself from
thought in that thought unfolded itself for him in dialogue),
he one day heard one of the philosophers, referring to that
thesis, express himself thus: 'This thesis does not belong to
any particular philosophy – it is a thesis from the eternal
philosophy, which anyone who wants to give himself to
philosophy must embrace.' Johannes noted that these words
clearly moved the audience; he himself felt blissfully
thrilled by the tremor of enthusiasm transmitted around. He
hastened home happier than Robinson Crusoe when he had
found Friday. On the way he repeated the words in order to
be sure that his memory should not deceive him.

The eternal philosophy, he said to himself, the eternal

philosophy – what does that mean? It is a glorious designation, and no designation can be too glorious for philosophy, but the more glorious a designation, the clearer and more obvious it presumably becomes. The eternal philosophy. Is it the philosophy which is indifferent to time? In that case it must be the most abstract philosophy; which in its abstraction has neither beginning nor end. It cannot be this, however, because the thesis speaks of a beginning. Is it the philosophy that has history within itself, the blessed transfiguration of philosophy's richly substantial life, which can best be compared with the transfiguration which every person expects in eternity when his life is over? If it is this, then strictly speaking one can only expect it. Already his soul began to be discouraged; those thrilling and powerful words were so faithless! Yet he still pinned his faith on the last part of the statement: 'Anyone who wants to give himself to philosophy must embrace this (the eternal philosophy).' But how one is to set about doing this, the speaker did not mention at all. What help was it to know that there is an eternal philosophy which everyone should embrace, if not everyone got to know how to set about doing this, or if nobody at all got to know, or at least if nobody in the audience got to know more than he? And yet it pained him; the words seemed to him so beautiful that he could not help dwelling on them, just as one sadly gazes at the flight of wild geese in the sky. Anyone who wants to belong to that world must join them, and yet no one had ever been seen flying with them.

The words had not helped him make progress, on the contrary they seemed to him on closer inspection to end precisely where he was about to begin before he had heard them, for that was precisely what he wanted to investigate – how the single individual must relate to that thesis, and therefore how the single individual should embrace philosophy. He could well perceive how little this edified him; for it could be deduced from it that he, a beginner, was at the place and was supposed to begin where the others had already ended. This was the similarity. It resembled a mathematical proposition, where the end agrees entirely with the beginning. For example, anyone beginning says, 'The square on the hypotenuse of a right-angled triangle is equal to the sum on the squares on the other two sides.' The one who ends says exactly the same, only adding *Quod erat demonstrandum* [which was to be demonstrated]. It pained him that the philosophers behaved in that way; it was shameful of them never to explain anything, for there might well be someone who needed an explanation. Johannes was again about to follow the drift of his own thoughts and the question was already hovering on his lips, when a new call sounded, for he heard one of the philosophers make a remark which seemed to him of the utmost importance. The thesis that 'philosophy begins with doubt' was a frequent general theme for discussion, but he now heard that the beginning of philosophy is three-fold: The *absolute* beginning is the concept that is also the end of the System, the concept of Absolute Spirit; the *objective* beginning is the concept of absolutely indeterminate being, the simplest definition that exists; the *subjective* beginning is the work of consciousness, by which it elevates itself to thinking or to positing the abstraction.

This remark made a salutary impression on Johannes. It seemed to him reliable and trustworthy, and even though it lacked the intoxicating power of enthusiasm, yet it seemed to possess clarity and coolness. What he found remarkable, however, was that this remark, which was supposed to shed light on the thesis about philosophy's beginning with doubt, declared to that end that the beginning of philosophy was threefold and named each part separately, yet none of these beginnings was described as philosophy's beginning with doubt. If he was to explain this by saying that philosophy had four beginnings, and the fourth was doubt, then he was in the awkward position of having to assume that the proposed explanation explained everything except that which he wanted to have explained. If any of the threefold beginnings referred to were the one in question, then he saw clearly that it must be the third, for consideration of philosophy's absolute and objective beginnings must be left to those who had already become philosophers. The subjective beginning on the contrary was certainly the one by which the single individual who had not been a philosopher could begin to be a philosopher. This was also that about which he asked, for he was not asking about the relation of this thesis to philosophy, but about his own relationship to this thesis and therefore his possible relation to philosophy.

'The subjective beginning', it was said, 'is the work of consciousness, by which it elevates itself to thinking or to positing the abstraction.' This seemed very beautiful to him, very elevating, but his consciousness was still not elevated by it. If this was the beginning he was talking about, then it was not clear to him why it now took on a positive form instead of the usual negative form. He could easily see that one could arrive at the same point by elevation or by doubt, but the continuity would be very different in each case. If one person, in order to philosophize, elevated himself above sensation, and another person doubted sensation for the same reason, they might perhaps both reach the same place, but the movement would be different; and the movement was precisely what Johannes was asking about. Moreover, since to elevate oneself is a positive principle, no historical consequence can be drawn from it with regard to a previous philosophy, as can be drawn from the principle of doubt. Can we then assert that these two expressions, to elevate oneself and to doubt, are identical? Why then use two expressions? Why explain the more difficult expression by an easier expression which in fact explains something very different and hence not what it should explain? The expression he heard repeated again and again was: Philosophy begins with doubt. The other expression he heard far more rarely. Must then the thesis be a misunderstanding and, on the other hand, the explanation be the thesis? That was quite unthinkable, and even if it were so it would presumably have its meaning as a thesis, and this would itself need explaining, for to say 'The beginning is the act whereby one begins' is a paltry sort of explanation. Further definition is necessary, explaining both the nature of the act and how the single individual becomes capable of carrying it out.

He therefore decided to begin again where he was on the point of beginning earlier, to follow the inclination of the question as he felt it in his soul.

(a) *How does the single individual who asserts that thesis relate himself to it?*

With this in mind, Johannes asked whether this thesis had in the temporal sense existed through all ages, so that everyone had known its content even though nobody had asserted it as a thesis. Had it the same validity as the sentence 'Man is mortal'? Did it but state something that people in all ages had done without being conscious of it? And was this something immediately inherent in human nature, like wonder, for example? For if nobody had ever explained what it is to wonder, every single person nevertheless would have done it. Or had the thesis existed through all ages in the eternal sense, but yet been discovered in time? Had it the same validity as mathematical propositions, which, when they are discovered, are discovered in their eternity? Would it continue to exist in the eternal sense through all ages, just as a philosophical thesis does? Was the personality of the discoverer of the thesis a matter of indifference after it was discovered, as is the case with mathematical and metaphysical theses? Was it of importance for the thesis that one should know the personality of the one who asserted it? With religious theses we certainly insist on having some knowledge of the speaker's personality; so also, to a certain extent, with ethical theses, for anybody can utter a religious and an ethical thesis, but it does not follow that in everyone's mouth it becomes a religious or ethical thesis, unless we assume that it makes no difference whether it was Christ who said he was the Son of God or anyone whatsoever, or that it makes no difference whether it was someone who really knew himself who said 'Know thyself'. The thesis certainly remains the same, and yet it becomes different – that is to say, in the one case it would become a thesis, in the other, chatter; whereas with a mathematical thesis it is entirely a matter of indifference whether it is Archimedes or tradition that asserts it, so long as it is asserted correctly. Personality in the one case means nothing, in the other, everything; just as in civil life anybody can be, in the formal sense, a guarantor, and yet it makes all the difference who the guarantor is.

What then must be the personality of the one who asserts this thesis? Must he have talent, and is this sufficient, so that if only he has talent he has authority to assert the thesis? To assert a mathematical proposition, mathematical talent is required. He who can state it shows that he has talent; and if one were to imagine the absurd situation that a person without talent could assert a mathematical thesis (which is always an absurdity because of the complete immanence of the talent in the presentation), the thesis would still retain its truth, its mathematical truth, that is, its essential truth; just as in ordinary life a bond payable to the bearer is just as valid whether a rich man or a poor man holds it, whether it is a thief or its rightful owner who possesses it. With religious and ethical propositions this is not the case. If one could teach a child of two a mathematical thesis, it would be essentially just as true in the mouth of a child as in the mouth of Pythagoras. But if one were to teach a child of two to say 'I believe in the existence of God', or 'Know thyself', nobody would take

him seriously. Is talent itself, then, not sufficient authority?
Do not religious and ethical truths require something else,
another kind of authority or, rather, what we really call
authority, for we certainly make a distinction between
talent and authority. If a person has sufficient talent to see
all the implications of such a thesis, and talent enough to
assert it, it does not follow that he himself believes it or
does it, and insofar as this is not the case, then he
transforms the thesis from a religious to a historical one, or
from an ethical to a metaphysical one.

Now it was clear to Johannes that insofar as there could not
be four beginnings to philosophy (and even if there had
been, the conclusion would remain the same) then the
thesis must belong to the subjective beginning. This is also
clear from the fact that it would be sheer nonsense to speak
of an objective doubt; for objective doubt is not doubt but
deliberation. The thesis therefore cannot, any more than any
other philosophical thesis, lay claim to mathematical
necessity, but neither can it lay claim to philosophical
necessity, as do all theses in the absolute and objective
philosophy. This thesis must therefore be such that whoever
would assert it must discover it, must have talent, must have
authority.

(b) *How does the single individual who receives this thesis
relate to the one who asserts it?*
Johannes saw at this point that some questions would turn
out to be the obverse side of the previous questions. With
these he could therefore be brief. He asked whether this
thesis, after it had been asserted, was forthwith valid

whether one intended it or not; like the statement 'Man is mortal'. Was it valid with such necessity that by denying it, one exposes oneself to the inverse conclusion, just as someone denying a mathematical proposition must be prepared to face the consequence that he has no head for mathematics? Was the thesis, like a mathematical thesis, indifferent as to whether many people or only a few assert it, neither gaining nor losing anything thereby?

The question he particularly focused on was: Can the thesis merely be stated, or must it actually be received? A mathematical thesis can essentially only be stated, for only when one has received it in such a way that he himself can state it, only then has he really received it – otherwise it does not exist for him. Johannes explained this as being due to the abstract nature of mathematics. Is that thesis, because of its negativity, not of the same kind? Does not the negative lack precisely that continuity without which no communication and no reception is conceivable? Is it not a deception to give the negative the appearance of possessing continuity? Is not negativity in the sphere of thought what evil is in the sphere of freedom, and thus, like evil, without continuity?

Can the thesis then not be received at all, but only asserted? Does everyone receive it in such a way that, in the moment he asserts it, it matters not whom he received it from or whether he received it at all, for he would not have received it until he himself asserted it? Can it be received; can the individual receive it from another; must it be believed? I mean that when I receive a thesis in faith, I am unable straightaway to grasp it or carry it out, but yet I receive it because I have faith in the person who asserts it. Perhaps the thesis is such that authority is required in those who assert it, and confidence and submission in those who are to receive it? Should it be believed in such a way that the individual does not do what the thesis said, but believes that the other has done it? Or perhaps one particular philosopher has doubted for all, as Christ suffered for all, so that now we have only to believe *this*, and do not have to doubt ourselves. In that case the thesis is certainly not asserted entirely correctly, for then philosophy does not for the single individual begin with doubt, but with the belief that philosopher so-and-so has doubted for him. Must the thesis be so trustfully appropriated that the single individual does what it says? Has the one who first asserts it doubted everything so completely that the single individual merely repeats his doubt, and makes the prescribed movements of doubt merely by believing in the propounder? Did there always, with every individual, come a new factor of doubt into the world for the next person? Regarding those things which the earlier individual had been able to doubt, ought one to believe that he had doubted enough, or ought one to doubt again?

The more Johannes thought about the matter the clearer it became to him that one cannot get into philosophy that way, for the thesis just destroyed the connection. He had read a story in an old saga about a knight who received from a troll a rare sword which, besides its other characteristics had also this, that as soon as one drew it forth, it craved blood. When the troll handed it to him, the knight's desire to see it was so great that he instantly drew it forth from its scabbard, and lo and behold! the troll had to bite the dust. Such it seemed to Johannes must be the case with that thesis. When one person said it to another, it became in the latter's hand a sword which must murder the first, however much it pained the second to repay his benefactor thus.

The pioneer who had first discovered that one must begin with doubt had not been in that predicament. Presumably he had begun as one begins a bold adventure, not knowing whether it would lead him to victory or to ruin. An individual who, by contrast, has to learn this from someone else is landed in this predicament, and if his teacher is not very quick, he must needs become a victim of his own teaching.

Such blood-thirsty ingratitude Johannes could not be party to. But although he gradually plucked up the courage for it, he could plainly see that there was a new difficulty, for as soon as he – against his will, he could say with a good conscience – had murdered his teacher, then he himself would become a teacher, would not profit in the least from his predecessors but, on the contrary, would have the prospect either of becoming the absolute monarch of philosophy (if, that is, he was the last to assert the thesis and had no successors, which would mean he was the monarch of all philosophers since he would be the only one) or else of ending in the same way as his great predecessors. *Aller Anfang ist schwer* [every beginning is difficult] – he had always thought the Germans were right about that, but this beginning seemed to him to be more than difficult, and to call this a beginning and dub it merely 'difficult' seemed to him like classifying a fox being skinned under the category of 'transition'.

Although these reflections were by no means encouraging to Johannes, he could not refrain from smiling now and then; for indeed smiles and tears often affect each other in a strange way. When he reflected that he, who was so innocent of blood that you might have thought him a girl rather than a man; he who had not the heart to hurt a fly – that he should be changed into a bloodthirsty Bluebeard who did not chop down corn but immortal philosophers for his food – then he felt how ridiculous a role he had come to play, and how the whole thing must be riddled with witchcraft. He had certainly grasped that a transformation must take place in someone when they became a philosopher – but such a transformation!

He decided therefore to let the sword remain for the time being in its sheath, and to continue being himself rather than becoming a philosopher on such terms.

Whatever else might be involved in that thesis and its relation to philosophy, this much he saw, that this beginning was a beginning whereby one remains outside philosophy, whether one assumes that philosophy would really endure even if the individual excluded himself from it by doubting, or whether one assumes that such a beginning destroys philosophy – which again would mean that one could not enter it.

The beautiful prospect which the thesis had opened for him had vanished. His only way out was to assume that this beginning was a beginning which preceded philosophy's own beginning. In that case, thesis number one was identical with thesis number two.

Chapter three

In order to philosophize
one must have doubted

It was, as the reader will remember, really the statement *de omnibus dubitandum est* that Johannes wanted to make the object of his deliberations. But first he wanted to encourage himself by exploring this statement's relation to philosophy. What he had discovered, after exhaustive labour, gave him little joy; for he was reduced to the paltry assertion that this statement lay outside philosophy and was a preparation. Yet even so, his efforts would not be without reward if by such preparation he made himself worthy of beginning philosophy later on.

In a certain sense there was nothing now to stop him from going on to that statement, for from it he surely must learn what he had to do, so that thereupon he might carry it out. Yet he thought it worth investigating what it could mean that philosophy should demand such preparation. And thesis number two gave him this opportunity.

That philosophy should demand such preparation seemed to him entirely in order – indeed it greatly appealed to him; his disposition, which was as humble as it was bold, wholly approved of it. Even if he had been fortunate enough to understand thesis number one, and to slip into philosophy with its help, he still would have been worried lest he had got there too easily, for to acquire something without difficulty was a paradox to his adventurous soul, which always preferred to seek out difficulties. He knew that such a preparation had been customary previously in the world. He knew that Pythagoras had commanded silence of his disciples, that Egyptian and Indian philosophers had used a similar period of probation; he knew that novices went through a long schooling before they were received into the Church. Indeed, the more important the mystery was into which you were being initiated, the stricter your probation. The ascetic monastic orders, the gigantic Jesuit order, were to him examples of this. No wonder then that philosophy in our age also required an ordeal! He also knew that it was not seemly for a disciple to criticize the master. What the master thinks good to command must be done with enthusiasm and complete confidence, however offensive or humiliating it may be. That Pythagoras had demanded silence Johannes could understand, for the disciple ought to keep quiet; that Diogenes required a would-be disciple to walk behind him carrying a pot he could well understand; that the novice had to stand outside the door, kneel when the others stood, stand when the others sat down, and undertake the coarsest work – all this seemed to him quite right, and he would never have hesitated to comply if it had been required of him. Yet he was for another reason a little hesitant about the preparation prescribed for him, because it did not seem to him to be sufficiently humble and modest.

He who doubts elevates himself above the person from whom he learns, and there is therefore no disposition which a teacher must frown on in his disciple so much as doubt. And yet it was doubt that was required of him; it was by doubting that he was to prepare to become a philosopher. Once again he was in a predicament. Perhaps, he thought, this is a pious fraud. Perhaps in this manner the disciple may be taught to rely upon the master, just as one lets a child burn itself at the fire, not warning it but encouraging it to do so, because experience is regarded as the best teacher. This explanation, however, did not satisfy him. Then he found another by observing that there is something elevated and noble in the conduct of philosophy. When the master positively commands the disciple to do something, then that is certainly easier for the disciple, because the teacher takes over the responsibility. But by this the disciple becomes an imperfect being, one who has his life in another person. But by imposing something negative upon the disciple, the teacher emancipates the disciple from himself, makes him just as great as himself. Indeed the relation of teacher and disciple is annulled. Johannes understood this clearly. 'I cannot even be sure', he said, 'whether doubt really is a preparation. I am delivered over to myself, I must do everything on my own responsibility. Even though I could have wished to remain a minor for a while longer, even though I could have wished that there were somebody to command me so that I might have the joy of obeying, even though I anxiously feel that I, so young, have come of age, even though I feel like a girl who has married too young – yet so it must be. The statement *de omnibus dubitandum est* is firmly fixed in my consciousness, and I will strive to think it through with all my strength and to do what it says with all my passion. Come what may, whether it brings me everything or nothing, makes me wise or mad, I will stake everything but I will not let go of the thought. My romantic dreams of being a disciple have vanished. Before I was allowed to be young I became old, and now I sail the open sea. The prospects I once dangled before my mind about the relation of this statement to philosophy are suffocated. I know nothing about the relation of this statement to anything else. I merely follow its path – 'like the one who rows a boat, I turn my back on my destination'.

Part two

Johannes tries to think *Propriis Auspiciis* [On his own Behalf] *De omnibus dubitandum est*

Introduction

Just as a fish, when it has snatched its prey from the scum of the water, dives down to the bottom of the sea, so Johannes was now alone with that statement in the depths of his soul. For a time he yielded to the various moods called forth by the mere possession of something whose true significance one still cannot perceive. He allowed himself to be variously swayed by his many thoughts about the difficulty of the task, about its entangling allurements, about the fruitless attempts he had already made, about the moments of triumph, about the romantic manner in which he would come to exist – in short he enjoyed the sweet joys and pains of a first love, for it is as Hippel somewhere says '*es geht mit den Wissenschaften wie mit der Liebe; die verstohlne ist die angenehmste* [in science as in love, furtiveness gives greatest pleasure]'.

As he gradually came more and more to himself, felt more and more the desire and the energy to tackle his task in more definite form, he strove to recall whether there had been anything in the talk of the philosophers that might be helpful. One does not undertake a journey round the world in the same way as a stroll. Not knowing the difficulties of the former, the soul takes refuge in some wistful, uplifting devotions, as courage and enthusiasm vie in romantic boldness with a certain anxiety. But although one thus hands oneself over to oneself, still nothing is more natural than that one should pay attention to the reports of those who have attempted the same thing. Johannes knew that he must not expect to find in the talk of the philosophers such complete information as a sailor has in his chart, but he also knew that the mind is not characterized by multiplicity, and that its movement is much more uniform.

Now when Johannes had racked his memory, he found himself in a curious position. For it became clear to him that there had hardly fallen a single word in the conversations of the philosophers about all the experiences and adventures in which one must be tried when setting out to doubt everything. And yet you would have expected to hear this. Indeed you might have thought that this would be their favourite topic, just as seafarers love to talk about the experiences they have been through, especially to those who have traversed the same seas. Johannes could have understood it if somebody or other had perjured himself by saying he had undergone such experiences when in fact he had not, but he hoped to be able to distinguish the experienced person from the parrots by the fervency of their statements. What was inexplicable, however, was that everybody remained silent. Could what they had seen be so dreadful that they dared not speak of it? Yet they were in the company of people who must have seen the same thing.

It was not completely true that Johannes had not heard a single word from the philosophizers about this matter, but when he revived in his memory the little he had heard, he was obliged to confess that it came to nothing, and that it was inevitable that the odd phrases he remembered should have discouraged him at the time. Thus on one occasion when there was talk of the significance of doubt as a preliminary to philosophy, Johannes was witness to the following statement: 'One must not waste time on doubting, but must just begin straight away on philosophy.' The audience seized upon this information with the same joy with which Catholics seize upon the proclamation of an indulgence. Johannes, however, felt so ashamed on the speaker's behalf that he wished himself miles away so that no one should see it on his face. 'Even an ordinary person', he said to himself, 'endeavours to do what he says, though it may happen that he does something else through ignorance, because he does not understand himself. Yet this cannot happen with the philosopher. But thus to say straight out that it is not worth taking pains to do what one at other times assures us one has done, deliberately leaving out what one usually emphasizes is a necessary condition – this is to hold both oneself and philosophy in contempt.' On another occasion, Johannes heard one of the philosophizers in whose statements people had special confidence express himself something like this: 'To doubt everything is no easy matter. It is not doubt about this, that or the other, about this thing or that, about something and something else; it is speculative doubt about everything, which is by no means an easy matter.' Johannes recalled how attentive he was made by the beginning of this lecture and how depressed he was at its conclusion, since he perceived that it did not say a single word. It would have been better if the speaker had said no more than these first words, for what followed said nothing, though it gave the appearance of saying something, and therefore it was odd that the lecture was not much longer; for when people talk like this they must have an endless amount to say.

Johannes then said goodbye to these philosophizers forever. Even though from time to time he heard some stray remark from them, he decided to heed them no more, since he had had so many sad experiences of how deceitful their words were. He followed now the method he had hitherto been wont to follow – that is, to make everything as simple as possible.

Chapter one

What is it to doubt?

1. How must existence be constituted in order that doubt can be possible?

When Johannes began to consider this, he of course perceived that if he demanded an empirical answer to this question, then life would offer such variety within the bounds of its total circumference that there would be only a confusing diffusion. Not only could that which evoked doubt in an individual be very different, but it could be the opposite, for if one were to preach doubt in order to awaken doubt in another, he might thereby evoke faith, just as faith, conversely, might evoke doubt. Because of this paradoxical dialectic, which, as he had noted previously, had no analogy in any sphere of knowledge, Johannes easily perceived that all empirical observation would lead to nothing. For all knowledge stands in a direct and immanent relation to its object and the knower, not in an inverse and transcendent relationship to a third. If he sought an answer to that question he must therefore take another route. He must try to discover *doubt's ideal possibility in consciousness*. This must of course remain the same, however different the phenomenon may be that gives rise to the doubt, since it explains the phenomenon's effect without itself being explained by the phenomenon. That which evokes doubt in the single individual may be as different as it likes; if there was not the possibility of doubt in the individual, nothing would be able to evoke it. Since, moreover, the difference in the phenomenon causing the doubt may be one of contrariety, the possibility must be all-embracing, and essential for human consciousness.

He then tried to orient himself in consciousness as it is in itself, as that which explains every individual consciousness without itself being an individual. He asked how consciousness would be constituted if it had doubt outside itself. There is consciousness in a child, but it has doubt outside itself. How then is the child's consciousness to be determined? It is actually quite indeterminate, which can also be expressed by saying that it is immediate. *Immediacy* is precisely *indeterminacy*. In immediacy there is no relation, for as soon as there is a relation immediacy is annulled. *Immediately, therefore, everything is true*; but this truth is in the next moment untruth, for *in immediacy everything is untrue*. If consciousness can remain in immediacy, then the question of truth is annulled.

How does the question of truth arise? Through untruth, for the moment I ask about truth, I have already asked about untruth. In the question of truth, consciousness is brought into relation with something else, and what makes this relation possible is untruth.

Which is first, immediacy or mediacy? That is a deceptive

question. It reminded him of the answer Thales is supposed to have given someone who asked whether night or day came into existence first: Night is one day earlier. Night, he said, is older by one day.

Cannot consciousness then remain in immediacy? This is a foolish question, for if it could there would be no consciousness at all. But how, then, is immediacy annulled? By mediacy, which annuls immediacy by *pre*-supposing it. What, then, is immediacy? It is reality. What is mediacy? It is words. How does the one annul the other? By giving expression to it, for that which is expressed is always *presupposed*.

Immediacy is reality; language is ideality; consciousness is contradiction. The moment I express reality, the contradiction is there, for what I say is ideality.

The possibility of doubt, then, lies in consciousness, whose very essence is a contradiction that is produced by, and itself produces, a duplexity.

Such a duplexity necessarily has two expressions. The duplexity is reality and ideality; consciousness is the relation. I can either bring reality into relation with ideality, or ideality into relation with reality. In reality alone there is no possibility of doubt; when I express it in language the contradiction is there, for I do not express it at all, but produce something else. Insofar as what is said was meant to express reality, I have brought this into relation with ideality; insofar as what is said is something produced by me, I have brought ideality into relation with reality. And so long as this exchange takes place without contact on either side, consciousness exists only according to its possibility. In ideality everything is just as perfectly true as in reality. Therefore, just as I can say that immediately everything is true, so can I also say that immediately everything is actual, for only at the moment when ideality is brought into relation with reality does *possibility* appear. In immediacy the most false and the most true are equally true; in immediacy the most possible and the most impossible are equally actual. So long as this exchange takes place without collision, consciousness does not really exist; and this tremendous fallacy causes no annulments. Reality is not consciousness, any more than ideality is, and yet consciousness does not exist without both, and this contradiction is the coming into existence of consciousness and its essence.

Before proceeding any further, Johannes considered whether what he here called consciousness was what is usually called reflection. In that respect he fixed his definition thus: reflection is the *possibility of the relation*, consciousness is *the relation, the first form of which is contradiction*. He soon noted that, as a result, the categories of reflection are always dichotomous. For example ideality and reality, soul and body, to recognize – the true, to will – the good, to love – the beautiful, God and the world, and so on, these are categories of reflection. In reflection, these touch each other in such a way that a relation becomes possible. The categories of consciousness, on the other hand, are trichotomous, as language itself indicates, for when I say, *I* am conscious of *this*, I mention a trinity. Consciousness is mind or spirit, and the remarkable thing is that when in the world of mind or spirit one is divided, it always becomes three and never two. Consciousness, therefore, presupposes reflection. If this were not so, it would be impossible to explain doubt. True, language seems to contest this, since in most languages, as far as he knew, the word 'doubt' is etymologically related to the word 'two'. Yet in his opinion this only indicated the presupposition of doubt, especially because it was clear to him that as soon as I, as spirit, become two, I am *eo ipso* three. If there were nothing but dichotomies, doubt would not exist, for the possibility of doubt lies precisely in that third which places the two in relation to each other. One cannot therefore say that reflection produces doubt, unless one expressed oneself backwards; one must say that doubt *pre*supposes reflection, though not in a temporal sense. Doubt arises through a relation between two, but for this to take place the two must exist, although doubt, as a higher expression, comes before rather than afterwards.

Reflection is the possibility of the relation. This can also be expressed as follows: Reflection is *disinterested*. Consciousness, however, is the relation and thereby the interest, a duality which is perfectly and with pregnant double meaning expressed by the word 'interest' (*interesse*, being between). All knowledge, therefore, which is disinterested (mathematics, aesthetics, metaphysics) is only the presupposition of doubt. As soon as the interest is annulled, doubt is not overcome but rather neutralized, and all such knowledge is but a retrogression. If anybody, therefore, imagines that he can overcome doubt with any so-called objective thinking, he is mistaken, for doubt is a higher form than all objective thinking, since it presupposes it but has something more, a third, which is interest or consciousness. In this respect the behaviour of the Greek sceptics seemed to Johannes far more consistent than the modern overcoming of doubt. They fully realized that doubt is due to interest, and therefore thought, quite consistently, that they could annul doubt by transforming interest into apathy. This procedure was consistent, whereas it is an inconsistency, apparently based on ignorance of what doubt is, which has motivated modern philosophy to want to overcome doubt systematically. Even if the System were absolutely complete; even if actuality exceeded expectations, still doubt would not be overcome – it begins first – for doubt is due to interest, and all systematic knowledge is disinterested. One can see from this that doubt is the beginning of the highest form of existence, because it can have everything else as its presupposition. The Greek sceptics excellently perceived that to talk about doubt is unreasonable when interest is annulled, but they probably would also have seen that it is a play on words to speak of an objective doubt. For let ideality and reality strive against each other to all eternity, so long as there is no consciousness, there is no interest, so long as there is no consciousness that has an interest in this struggle, there is no doubt – but let them be reconciled, and doubt can continue unabated.

Consciousness is, then, the relation, a relation whose form is contradiction. But how does consciousness discover the contradiction? If the fallacy mentioned earlier could remain, that ideality and reality communicated with each other in all innocence, consciousness would never emerge, for consciousness emerges precisely through the collision, just as it presupposes the collision. Immediately there is no collision, but mediately it is there. As soon as the question of a *repetition* arises, the collision is there, for repetition is only conceivable of what existed before.

In reality as such there is no repetition. This is not because everything is different; not at all. If everything in the world were absolutely identical, still in reality there would be no repetition, because reality is only 'in the moment'. If the world, instead of being beauty, were nothing but equally large, undiversified boulders, there would still be no repetition. Through all eternity, in every moment, I would see a boulder; but there would be no question as to whether it is the same one as I had seen before. In ideality alone there is no repetition, for the Idea is and remains the same, and as such it cannot be repeated. When ideality and reality touch each other then repetition appears. When, for example, I see something in the moment, ideality intervenes and will explain that it is a repetition. Here is the contradiction, for that which is, is also in another mode. That the external is, that I can see, but in the same instant I bring it into relation with something else which also is, something that is the same and which will also explain that the other is the same. Here is a redoubling; here there is the question of repetition.

Ideality and reality therefore collide – in what medium? In time? That is of course an impossibility. In eternity? That also is of course an impossibility. In what then? In consciousness – there is the contradiction. The question is not disinterested, as though one were asking whether all existence is only an image of the Idea, and whether, if not, visible existence is a repetition in an emaciated sense. Here the question is rather one of a repetition in consciousness, therefore of recollection. Recollection involves the same contradiction. Recollection is not ideality; it is ideality which has been. It is not reality; it is reality which has been, which again is a double contradiction, for ideality cannot by definition have been, and the same holds, by definition, of reality.

From an aesthetic point of view
Philosophy, art and the senses

Edited by Peter Osborne

Contemporary visual art stands on the ruins of beauty. What is the place of the aesthetic in the experience of such art? And how has it changed in the two hundred years since the emergence of the modern conception of art as the object of a distinctive kind of pleasure in form? The essays in this volume, by philosophers and art theorists from Britain, France, Germany and the USA, investigate the changing role of the aesthetic in art. In writing that is both lucid and challenging, the contributors make clear that the importance a society places on art and the aesthetic is a barometer of its very health.

Contributors

Sylviane Agacinski

David Batchelor

Jay Bernstein

Howard Caygill

Alexander Garcia Düttmann

Christoph Menke

Mandy Merck

Peter Osborne

Jacques Rancière

Jonathan Rée